Commanding the Storms to

HAVE A

JESUS

FILLED

AMERICA®

ROY CHAPMAN

DEDICATION

This book is dedicated to my children and their families. My prayer is that Jesus will always have the first place in your lives.

ACKNOWLEDGMENTS

Most important, I would like to thank my Lord Jesus Christ for allowing me to do His divine work. Without Jesus, there would not be an Extraordinary Place of Peace for me to dwell each day. Furthermore, I give thanks to my Lord Jesus Christ for choosing and trusting me to be His messenger. His presence fills my life in every place.

To Nancy and Bryan Clement, my special friends, I am honored that you are a vital part of this ministry. I appreciate your faithful prayers and love.

To co-laborers in this ministry, Deborah and Randy Elum, I thank you for supporting, encouraging, praying for, and loving me. Thank you, Deborah, for your many unique contributions to this book. Your insightful vision inspired me to remain persistent in completing this project. I appreciate your creative efforts and the countless hours that you spent to bring this to fruition.

To all of the ministry partners, who are faithful in your love and service, I give thanks to you. Your prayers and support help me fulfill the calling that God has given to me.

I extend my gratitude to Tracie Spradlin for her assistance in this endeavor. I appreciate your honest opinions and help with the many different aspects of this book. Your encouragement, love, and prayers are always important to me.

To Brenda Phillippe, thank you for your inspiration and faithfulness.

To Rev. Larry and Jana Hinson, Rev. Joe and Pauline Moles, and Linda and the late Rev. Larry Joe Wright; my special friends, you are very important to me. I am grateful to one of my dearest friends, the late Kenny Hinson, who encouraged me to answer the calling of God on my life.

I am grateful to those, too many to name, who have impacted my life throughout the years. Everyone is known by the Lord and shall receive their reward from Him (Luke 6:23).

Pledge of Allegiance

I pledge allegiance to the Flag of the United States of America, and to the Republic for which it stands, one Nation under God, indivisible, with liberty and justice for all.

Contents

Introduction 13

1. America is at a Crossroad 15

2. One Nation Under God 25

3. Built on a Firm Foundation 35

4. Revive Us Again 47

5. Commanding the Storms 59

6. Moving America Forward 67

7. Prayers for the Nation 77

INTRODUCTION

Our freedom is under attack all around us. Amazingly enough, it is not from a hostile or foreign enemy. The attack is right here in our own backyard. Americans who do not believe in Christ are hard at work, trying to limit the freedom we have as Christians to openly express our beliefs. Whether we realize it or not, year after year, they are restricting the use of Jesus' name. They are telling us there is no room for Him. Unfortunately, they are slowly shutting Him out of our country, government, communities, schools, celebrations, and now, even some churches.

Our founding fathers or forefathers fought for what is right, and we have to do likewise. To do likewise, we have to get out of our comfort zone. We can no longer afford to sit back and allow anything else to happen to take Christ out of America. We must come out of this spiritual slumber, rise up, stand together, and take action.

The future of America requires that we take a stand for our rights and the rights of future generations in this country. Generations to come will be able to say that their forefathers, that's you and me, took a stand for freedom. They can continue to have the freedom to preach, teach, and speak the name of Jesus, if we continue to fight for it. We, as God's people, must stand up and acknowledge the name of Jesus like never before. Yes, it takes strength, effort, and even courage to stand for what we believe in. We must be committed to our Lord Jesus Christ and the next generation to *Have a Jesus Filled America.*

CHAPTER 1

AMERICA
IS AT A
CROSSROAD

"If my people, who are called by my name, will humble themselves and pray and seek my face and turn from their wicked ways, then I will hear from heaven, and I will forgive their sin and will heal their land."

2 CHRONICLES 7:14 (NIV)

Have you ever had an uninvited guest in your home? Most of us have experienced this, and it is usually not a big problem at all. But there are times when we may be inconvenienced by such a visit because we have to change our plans to accommodate them. Since they are our guests, even though uninvited, we have to try to make them comfortable, right?

What if while you were eating, they removed your plate from the table? Then, while you were watching your favorite program on television, they turned the channel. Or, without your permission, they went into your bedroom, took your clothes out of the closet, threw them away, and put their clothes in place of your clothes. All because, they disapprove of what you eat, how you dress, or anything that you watch. They did all of that because your lifestyle made them uncomfortable. As funny as this may seem, this is exactly what is happening to the Christians in America. That is how America has been run, oftentimes. When ungodly laws are passed, or as ungodly people are elected, it means America is at a crossroad. When people sin and it is accepted, America is at a crossroad.

Do you know what a crossroad is? A crossroad is where two or more roads meet, or it is a critical turning point. When you come to a crossroad, you can turn left, right, around, or keep straight ahead. There is a point where you are forced to make a choice.

If America is at a crossroad, why don't we head in the right direction? Maybe it is because we don't want to be viewed as strange or a troublemaker. Worse yet, maybe it's because we have become "set in our ways," or "comfortable" with the way things are going. We must realize that as a nation, it does not matter if we have been wrong for 20 years, if we are wrong, we are just wrong. We are supposed to be the sign that point the way to Jesus and away from sin and destruction.

What's going on within the land in which we live concerns all of us. The Body of Christ can't afford to stand idly by and let it happen. We should be the sign, that warns the ungodly of what is ahead, if they do not turn to Jesus.

> *"If my people, which are called by my name, shall humble themselves, and pray, and seek my face, and turn from their wicked ways; then I will hear from heaven, and I will forgive their sin, and will heal their land."*
>
> 2 CHRONICLES 7:14 (NIV)

We need to speak out about what is going on and not allow our voices to be silenced. If we allow Jesus Christ to be taken out of America, then the spirit of the antichrist will take charge. If we want to, *"Have a Jesus Filled America,"* we have to develop an attitude of, "Enough is enough!" We have to take a bolder stand that Jesus Christ is Lord in America.

We understand clearly through the Word of God in 2 Chronicles 7:14 that as a nation, we need to take a stand for righteousness over our land.

God says that if His people would humble themselves, pray, seek His face, and turn from their wicked ways, that He will hear them. The problem is, we are trying to get everybody else to be humble, instead of first, humbling ourselves. As a people, we have a problem giving up all of our sins. But if we would do what God asks of us, He will forgive our sins and He will heal our land.

Things are changing in America right before our eyes. Ungodly laws are being passed. People can't pray openly at many school events. Christian symbols, including the Bible, are being removed from public buildings. I'm astonished by what's going on in this country and how fast things are happening; things that are not for the good of this country. It is very apparent in our society; that we need more godly people in public office especially, when we see that elected officials can take prayer out of schools, remove the Ten Commandments displays from public buildings, and more.

It's happening right where we live; in our homes, our bodies, in the work place, and even in our business affairs. Our land needs to be healed, and the only way, is for God's people to humble themselves and pray. God is not talking about sinners. He is talking about His people turning from their wicked ways. God wants His people to be separated from unclean things.

You might ask yourself, *What can I do?*

One way you can demonstrate your commitment to your country and to God is to vote and pray. You need to believe that every time you vote, you are making a difference. Your vote matters as to what goes on in this country. If you will start acting like it, talking like it, and believing that you are making a difference, you will begin to see it. We need godly men and women to be presidents, governors, senators, representatives, mayors, and other elected officials. We must pray to get those elected officials who can hear from God, receive divine direction, and make righteous judgments or decisions.

How do you vote for the right person? The Word of God says that the Lord orders your steps (Proverbs 16:9). If the Lord orders your steps, then the Lord is ordering your decisions. If you are obedient and allow that to happen, then you are voting for the right person. The Bible confirms this in 1 Timothy 2:1-2:

> "I exhort therefore, that, first of all, supplications, prayers, inter-cessions, and giving of thanks, be made for all men; For kings, and for all that are in authority; that

we may lead a quiet and peaceable life in all godliness and honesty."

We are still commanded by God to pray for those that are in authority over us. We should pray for those who are in office whether we voted them in, or not. It does not matter if they are Republican, Democrat, or Independent; whether they are Catholics, Christians, or Jews. If our hope is in a person, we will be disappointed in some of their decisions no matter who is elected. Our part of taking a stand is to vote and pray. Remember, your hope of maintaining a "Jesus Filled America" is not in who is elected to public office, although we should elect the right people. Our hope must always be in Jesus Christ.

In America, what has happened all through our society and our churches, is little by little, we have gotten farther and farther from Jesus.

All through society, you can find people who have turned away from the Lord. Only the people of God have the power to turn that trend around. I know the politicians get most of the blame, but the biggest blame is on us as Christians. Christians need to be united. We must be determined to stand on the Word of God because, united we stand and divided, we will fall.

PRAYER FOR OUR ELECTED OFFICIALS

Father, in the name of Jesus, we lift up our President and every branch of the government. As great decisions are being made that affect us, our children, and the future generations to come, we pray that You give our leaders wisdom and knowledge. Let them stand for righteousness.

We pray that the Holy Ghost will direct them in the things of God, and that this nation will remain as one nation, under God. We make a declaration that we are in faith and unity, believing that You are Lord over America. We declare that whatever changes are needed; that may even mean putting new people in office, so be it. In the name that's above every name.

In the name of Jesus, Amen!

CHAPTER 2

ONE NATION UNDER GOD

"And Elijah came unto all the people, and said, How long halt ye between two opinions? if the LORD be God, follow him: but if Baal, then follow him. And the people answered him not a word."

1 KINGS 18:21

When I was 13 years old, I lived with my uncle Gerald Chapman and his wife. I remember my uncle struggled just to make a living and put food on the table. During that time, beef liver was really cheap, so my aunt would cook and serve it every single day. She served it every day because it was what Uncle Gerald could afford. Even though I did not like liver at all, that did not matter. They told me I had to eat what was on the table. I complained for a while by way of my actions. Finally, I got the message, when I realized that I did not have a choice in the matter. So, I learned to tolerate it and eventually learned to like it.

BECOMING WHAT YOU EAT

Too often, Christians just accept whatever is on the table. We are shown how to act ungodly and it is being served to us day after day. It's being served to us every day on the television, the radio, the Internet, billboard signs, etc. When we feed upon doubt, disbelief, unclean images, fear, negative attitudes, discouragement, and idol worship, we become what we eat. In other words, we become contaminated with the things of this world. As a nation, we are at the place where we have begun tolerating it. In some cases, we have learned to like it. We become so full of trash; we do not want to eat the Bread of Life. – Jesus

There are some people who think that anything and everything goes in America since this is the land of freedom. They want to do anything, watch anything, and worship anything. But let's set the record straight, without Jesus, there is no freedom.

Many people enjoy the freedom and benefits that America has to offer. America has welcomed them with open arms to partake of the liberty that was established by our forefathers. This liberty was paid for with their lives, finances, and future. America is a

> *"Even so faith, if it hath not works, is dead, being alone."*
>
> JAMES 2:17

prosperous country because this nation was established upon the Word of God. However, some people do not care or know that godly men founded this country upon godly principles. They want the Living God kicked out so they can serve idol gods. The Bible definitely says in Psalm 115:4-8:

> "Their idols are silver and gold, the work of men's hands. They have mouths, but they speak not: eyes have they, but they see not: They have ears, but they hear not: noses have they, but they smell not: They have hands, but they handle not: feet have they, but they walk not: neither speak they through their throat. They that make them are like unto them; so is every one that trusteth in them."

The Bible states in James 2:17 that, "Even so faith, if it hath not works, is dead, being alone."

Freedom under God is the foundation that this nation was based on. Our founding fathers believed as long as they were obedient, listened, and obeyed God; they could stay free men. As long as this nation allows God to be the foundation, it will remain a strong and prosperous land.

Unfortunately, we are losing more of our freedom as Christians. Anytime God is kept out; we will lose more of our freedom to display our faith. Over the years, we have lost the freedom to talk about Him in public schools, at our jobs, and even at some governmental ceremonies. When we have the wrong people in office, they do not support laws that benefit Christian principles. That means we need to put action to our faith. We need to take a stand and become more involved in the decisions that shape America.

WE NEED A CHANGE

We need to vote in people that are God-fearing, who will stand up for godly principles. Romans 8:1 declares, "There is therefore now no condemnation." In other words, there is no guilt – to them which are in Christ Jesus who walk not after the flesh, but after the Spirit. When we walk after the Spirit, we're walking according to the Word of God, which guarantees help from the Holy Spirit and victory. Then, we are able to walk according to the law of the Spirit of Life in Christ Jesus, who has made us free from the law of sin and death.

The world is becoming very religious. There is even a new movement that talks about "God." The question is, are they talking about our God? Or false gods, that have filtered in to America? We have to know that the Lord Jesus Christ is the only way to our God, the God of Abraham, Isaac, and Jacob.

While visiting Orlando, Florida, I saw a billboard that read, "Jews, Christians, and Muslims – One God – Many Paths – Let's Talk." God does not want us to be deceived. If you reject Jesus, you reject God. It is as simple as that. The Bible states very clearly that there is only one way to heaven and that is through God's Son, Jesus. Therefore, we are declaring that Jesus is Lord over America!

If this nation continues to deviate from godly principles, it will be headed in the wrong direction just as the nation of Judah and Israel experienced during the reign of King Solo-

> *"For it came to pass, when Solomon was old, that his wives turned away his heart after other gods: and his heart was not perfect with the LORD his God, as was the heart of David his father."*
>
> 1 KINGS 11:4

mon. King Solomon disobeyed God by allowing his wives to worship foreign gods instead of the Living God. In 1 Kings 11:1-2, we find the story:

> "But King Solomon loved many strange women, together with the daughter of Pharaoh, women of the Moabites, Ammonites, Edomites, Zidonians, and Hittites; Of the nations concerning which the Lord said unto the children of Israel, Ye shall not go in to them, neither shall they come in unto you: for surely they will turn away your heart after their gods: Solomon clave unto these in love."

God commanded Solomon not to marry foreign women who did not believe in the God of Israel. But he did not listen to what

God had spoken to him. Solomon married many heathen women and allowed them to introduce idolatry and wickedness into Israel. The Lord was angry with him because his heart was turned from the God of Israel. He also taxed people too heavily and drafted them mercilessly for public service as well as for the army. Because of his oppression and growing sin, the people of God were ready to revolt against him at the end of his reign.

As people of God, we too are ready to revolt. We will not allow our freedom to be taken away. As we join our faith together as a mighty army of believers, we are ready for our generation to see changes in this land.

PRAYER FOR CHANGE

Father, in the name of Jesus, we thank You for Your amazing grace, for it endures forever. We ask You to minister through us, for You are the only one that can touch our hearts and lives. We ask that our vessels be used for Your purpose and not our own. We ask for the convicting power of the Holy Ghost to move in such a mighty way, that our hearts will be changed and have a deep desire to pray and seek Your will for America. We ask that the anointing power of the Holy Ghost flow through, on, and over us. Father, we give You the glory and the praise.

In the name of Jesus, Amen!

CHAPTER 3

BUILT ON A FIRM FOUNDATION

"He is like a man which built an house, and digged deep, and laid the foundation on a rock: and when the flood arose, the stream beat vehemently upon that house, and could not shake it: for it was founded upon a rock."

LUKE 6:48

I participated in various sports including football, track, and boxing when I was in high school. I understood the importance of keeping my body in shape by maintaining a daily exercise regimen. My regimen involved running, weight lifting, and climbing ropes. If it had to do with building up my body and making it stronger, I did it. I knew that training was the foundation to winning. The same is true about faith.

When you put faith to work, it will increase. Your confidence in God will grow stronger and stronger. The Word will build you up so that you can come out the victor. You will have confidence and be fully persuaded that what God has promised, He will perform.

STRENGTH FOR THE NATIONS

Through the centuries, America had to overcome many storms; wars, presidential assassinations, stock market crashes, natural disasters, and bombings, just to name a few.

Although storms have come and gone, America still stands strong and unshaken. The only reason that we have survived is because our nation is built on the foundation that Jesus Christ is Lord over America. Our forefathers established this nation upon the Word of God. They believed that America should always remain one nation under God. They named our country "United States" because they understood as Christians, the power of agreement. They knew much could be accomplished when they were unified to establish a country where people were free to worship God and have the opportunity to prosper.

A FOUNDATION OF FAITH

Does America really have a godly heritage? Most of our founding fathers who worked on the Constitution were members of an Orthodox church, and many of them were evangelical Christians. Together, they estab-lished a foundation of faith. Godly principles were not just taught at church but at home and in schools. We need to go back to the godly principles that they set up in the beginning. We must go back to godly principles in every area of America.

If you want something, you are going to go after it. If you want freedom, you have to go after it. If a nation is to stay free, it must have people who will fight for it. That is why we have a military, to keep America free. Thank God for the military and the freedom that we have in this country. We are a free country, but freedom was and still is not cheap. Men and women have shed blood in the past, as well as presently, in order for us to be able to enjoy the liberties of freedom.

As I traveled to Orlando, Florida, I stopped in Mobile, Alabama to rest. I checked into a hotel for the night. During the night, someone broke a window out of my vehicle. I thanked God that they did not take anything because the car was loaded with my clothes and many other personal items.

The next morning when I found out that it was broken, I decided to go to a dealership to have the window replaced. After the hotel management had learned about the situation, a gentleman working at the hotel volunteered to escort me there in his car. As I walked outside, I saw on his license plate, a sign that read, "Retired from the Military." I took the time to honor him and thank him for his commitment to America. He was amazed that I thanked him for his service to our country. That was the least I could do to show my appreciation for his service to America. I told him that I am thankful for every person that ever served in any branch of the military.

As Christians, we too are in the military. We are in God's military. We have an obligation to this nation, and God, to stand and fight for the rights that the Lord Jesus Christ has provided for us. He sacrificed His life for us to be free in every area of our lives.

To have a "Jesus Filled America," we must have a Jesus filled people. If we have a strong people in God, we will have a strong nation, in God. The Word of God says in Galatians 5:1 to, "Stand fast therefore in the liberty wherewith Christ hath made us free, and be not entangled again with the yoke of bondage." In other words, do not let yourself be burdened down with sin. So many in America live in a free country but are in bondage to sin, debt, sickness, disease, and wrong relationships. The good news is that as Christians, we

> *"It is for freedom that Christ has set us free. Stand firm, then, and do not let yourselves be burdened again by a yoke of slavery."*
>
> GALATIANS 5:1 (NIV)

can fight for others who are in bondage to become free as well.

God is calling us back to Jesus and back to the cross. Many churches don't want to say anything about the cross. Everything comes to us because of the blood of Jesus. Many of us have been set free by the shed blood of Jesus Christ.

The blood makes us whole, saves our soul, breaks every bondage, and every chain in our lives. It's time to go back to the cross so we can truly bring Jesus back into our lives. It is time we give Him first place.

The Word of God says in Psalm 24:1 that, "The earth is the Lord's, and the fulness thereof; the world, and they that dwell therein." That means, everything you are and own, belongs to God; your car, bank account, house, and even you.

"What? know ye not that your body is the temple of the Holy Ghost which is in you, which ye have of God, and ye are not your own? For ye are bought with a price: therefore glorify God in your body, and in your spirit, which are God's." 1 Cor 6:19-20

Thank God that as Christians, we have the weapons to defend and protect the spirit man. We fight to protect our salvation, our walk with God, and our purpose and destiny for our lives. When we commit our heart and life to Him, we have been given our freedom. It is up to us to make sure that we stay free. The Scripture says in 1 Timothy 6:12, "Fight the good fight of faith, lay hold on eternal life, whereunto thou art also called, and hast pro-fessed a good profession before many witnesses."

God's people are the ones who are supposed to set the example of righteousness. The way you live before others is important because people are looking for the right path. You are lighting the path for others to see the right way to go and know the right things to do. If you do that, they will want what you have.

In John 8:34 (NIV), Jesus replied, "Very truly I tell you, everyone who sins is a slave to sin." A slave is not a permanent member of the family, but a son is a part of the household forever. The greatest freedom is knowing the truth. That means that knowing Jesus is the greatest freedom you will ever experience. You never have to be in bondage to sin.

Jesus crucified, is the answer to problems today and forever. Jesus Christ coming and being crucified for us was the answer for everyone to have freedom from sin. In John

8:47 (NLT), "Anyone who belongs to God listens gladly to the words of God."

Do you listen gladly to the words of God? Then, you must belong to God, or you must have a desire to belong to God. The closer you are to Almighty God, the more you will want to be in the Word and live according to His teachings.

When you know Jesus Christ is the Lord of your life, and He's your personal Savior, you have freedom from all your sins. They are washed away and your sins are forgiven.

Galatians 5:1 (NLT), says: "So Christ has truly set us free. Now make sure that you stay free, and don't get tied up again in slavery to the law." Christ died to set us free from sin, all the regulations of the law, guilt, and shame. Jesus came to take away the condemnation from those that are in Christ Jesus. Christ didn't die so you could be free to do your own thing. If you're in Christ, there is no such thing as your own thing.

If you are not careful, the devil will try to come in and talk to you about your past. He will try to put condemnation on you again. Don't allow the devil to drag up your past. Don't let sins from your past hold you in bondage. The Lord has forgotten every one of them and washed them away. He doesn't remember a single one of them.

The world needs what we have, the light and joy of Jesus Christ. As godly people, we have to allow the light and joy of Jesus to shine so bright that it should make people wonder what we have. Then, we will have an opportunity to witness to them about Jesus.

PRAYER FOR PROTECTION
OF
THE MILITARY

Father, in the name of Jesus, I thank You for all the men and women in every branch of the military. I give You praise for them. I thank You for what You are doing in their lives by the Spirit of the Living God. I pray that the ministering Spirit of God be disbursed to them right now wherever they are.

Thank You, Lord, that You put someone in their path that will minister to and encourage them. If they don't know You, we pray that they will be convicted of their sins, repent, and give their heart to You.

I pray for Your protection over them. I ask for the safety of Your hand and that the blood of Jesus be upon them and over them. I ask that they have high favor and that they be victorious in every situation in their lives, according to Your Word. Let Your will be done in their lives and the lives of their families. I lift them up to You with thanksgiving and praise. I pray that You are moving on their behalf even right now.

In the name of Jesus, Amen!

CHAPTER 4

REVIVE US AGAIN

"Wilt thou not revive us again: that thy people may rejoice in thee?"

PSALM 85:6

God made a promise to Abraham in Genesis 12:3. He promised him that He would bless them that bless Abraham and curse them that curse Abraham. Through Him, all the families of the earth will be blessed. We are Abraham's seed, so that promise is ours as well.

Think about how blessed we are. Reflect on how far we have come as a nation in a short period of time because of the Lord. It is so important in these changing times that we don't let the times change us.

For example, I refuse to shop at a store that doesn't support Christian values. My money just won't go there. I am blessed and where I go is blessed. Therefore, I don't want to bless a place that is against God and His people.

There is something wrong when American companies can purchase from countries that do not believe that Jesus is Lord. They are buying foreign products, hiring foreign workers, or contracting foreign companies to produce their products. The foreign companies can produce goods and services at lower prices and sell them to the American companies for less than if those products were made in America. Because of this trend, many American companies that make their products in America can't compete with them. Many of them have gone out of business and caused American workers to lose their jobs.

There is something wrong when Christians will not rise up and stand against this type of trend; or when Christians continue to purchase goods and services from companies that do not care about our beliefs.

ONE PERSON CAN MAKE A DIFFERENCE

Back in the 1960s, schools all over America opened each day with prayer and the Pledge of Allegiance, proclaiming that this is the "Lord's Day." Everyone heard the principal or assistant principal's voice as they prayed for direction in their lives and that of their students. After prayer, the Pledge of Allegiance was given, thus making another declaration that America is under God. It taught students to honor both; God and America. Now, for the most part, this has been eliminated in public schools. It took one woman, who did not believe in Jesus to start a movement that was responsible for having prayer removed from public schools.

I recall a relative of mine saying, "That will never happen in America."

It did happen. It happened because Christians did not stand up for what was right. In America, the Bible was once used as a textbook. The sad truth now is, if a child takes a Bible to a public school, he or she can get in trouble. In public schools, teachers can fail a student just for submitting a paper that has the name, Jesus Christ, written on it. Principals are even allowed to expel students if they continue to reference His name. This is happening all over America.

Too long, the Christian church has simply sat back and said, "That's just another sign that the Lord is coming back." Yes, that is another sign, but realize something, He did not put us here to sit around and wait on heaven.

We need to wake up and realize that our activities today have a direct effect in the lives of our children and our children's children. We don't want the next generation to look back and ask, "Why didn't you do something?"

You have to be determined that you will not sit back, lie back, or turn back. Stand up for what you believe. Don't focus on what you can't do; focus on what you can do.

God commands us to be strong and courageous like in Joshua 1:6-7:

> *"Then Peter opened his mouth, and said, Of a truth I perceive that God is no respecter of persons."*
>
> ACTS 10:34

"Be strong and of a good courage: for unto this people shalt thou divide for an inheritance the land, which I sware unto their fathers to give them. Only be thou strong and very courageous, that thou mayest observe to do according to all the law, which Moses my servant commanded thee: turn not from it to the right hand or to the left, that thou mayest prosper whithersoever thou goest."

NOT JUST ORDINARY

You may feel like you are just an ordinary person. You may have even wondered how God could ever use a person like you to make a difference. You have to understand that God uses ordinary people to perform or accomplish extraordinary tasks. Each time that God was ready to take action on the earth, He used an ordinary person just like you. Every day that you go to work, or whatever you do, if you allow Jesus Christ to shine in your life, you are making a difference. This is not about age, race, or gender. It is about what Christ can do through you and in you if you let Him.

God used Noah to save his family from the flood. By saving his family, Noah saved the human race from being totally destroyed. He used Joseph to save many nations during the seven years of famine. God used Moses to bring the Israelite nation out of Egyptian bondage. God used Mary to give birth to the Savior of the world. He even used Esther, a young Jewish girl who had the favor of God on her life.

King Ahasuerus made Esther a queen be-cause of God's favor on her life. Being queen allowed her to fit into the perfect plan of God. It was God's plan and timing to bring her to the kingdom. God knew of the evil plan that Haman had to destroy the Jews. Because she was in a position of influence, there came a time when she had to make a decision to either be silent, or speak out against a wicked plot by Haman. If she spoke out, she could have possibly been killed. However, if she remained silent, it could have meant the death of her people. Her cousin Mordecai gave her this advice in Esther 4:13-14:

"Then Mordecai commanded to answer Esther, Think not with thyself that thou shalt escape in the king's house, more than all the Jews. For if thou altogether holdest thy peace at this time, then shall there enlargement and deliverance arise to the Jews from another place; but thou and thy father's house shall be destroyed:

and who knoweth whether thou art come to the kingdom for such a time as this?"

God is not a respecter of persons, therefore, as He was with Moses and Joshua, He will be with you. Each one of them were ordinary people willing to be utilized in the plan of God. Like Queen Esther, you are here to make a difference. You are here in America for such a time as this. The key to doing extraordinary tasks for God is to be a willing vessel.

DANCE WITH THE ONE THAT BRUNG YA

There is a saying in the south that goes like this, "Dance with the one that brung ya." It means that if someone brought you to the dance, you dance with him or her only, and no one else. As a nation, we are dancing with so many other people that we have forgotten who built this nation. Let us not forget that it was God alone that brought us.

Let's stand together. Let's rise up like never before with our prayers and support to let the enemy know that we are not turning back. We are not turning to the left or to the right. We are pressing towards the mark of the higher calling. We will *Have a Jesus Filled America* now and for every generation to come.

PRAYER FOR REVIVAL

Father, in the name of Jesus, we give You thanks that revival is hitting America, the government, the military, the schools, and is spreading across this land. We make a declaration of faith that revival is happening right now. We make a declaration that prayer comes back into schools. We are believing for the Holy Ghost to help this message of salvation to spread.

We stand in agreement that we are going back to the things of God. Father, we give You honor, we give You glory, we give You praise, and we give You thanks. We stand in the gap for this country.

In the name of Jesus, Amen!

CHAPTER 5

COMMANDING
THE
STORMS

"And they said unto him, Ask counsel, we pray thee, of God, that we may know whether our way which we go shall be prosperous."

JUDGES 18:5

I realize there are things that happen to all of us. That's life, and it sometimes causes us to get stuck in those situations or storms. There will be times during our lives when we feel like there is nothing we can do, or we don't know what to do. So, we are just stuck.

When people get stuck, they often times seek counsel from ungodly people, instead of from God. The same thing is happening to Christians in America. When situations and burdens come against their lives, they start murmuring and complaining. Some even take counsel from ungodly people because they are not willing to listen to God. Therefore, they too are doing the wrong things and getting stuck. Complainers are always unhappy about something. Instead of praying and interceding for people in trouble, they will find something to complain about.

It is real easy for us to join in, instead of praying and seeking God for answers. So, we join in with the complainers. Do you know what happens when we join in with them? That same complaining and criticizing spirit tries to attach itself to us. Then, we can get stuck like the children of Israel did.

CHOOSE TO BELIEVE

In Exodus, the Lord wanted Moses to take His people from the bondage of Egypt to a land of freedom and abundance. When they started off, everyone was so excited. Yet, every time they were faced with difficult circumstances in the journey, they felt like God was not going to take care of them. When they felt stuck, they started complaining and murmuring against Moses.

They were saying the wrong things and ended up with exactly what they were saying. Their conversations were about how they would be destroyed and end up dying out in the desert. God got tired of listening to what they were saying and gave them exactly what they said. They ended up not going to the Promised Land because of their own words. Many of them were stuck in the storm of doubt and disbelief and never received the promise of a better life.

STANDING STRONG THROUGH STORMS

All through the Bible, there are people who chose to believe God and stand firm through the storms of life. In spite of their current circumstances, they made a decision of faith. They allowed God to work out His perfect will in their lives. They chose to be used mightily for the kingdom of God even if it cost them

> *"Not that I speak in respect of want: for I have learned, in whatsoever state I am, therewith to be content."*
>
> PHILIPPIANS 4:11

their lives.

Paul was such a person who experienced many hardships in his life as a believer. In 2 Corinthians 11:25, Paul shares some of his hardships saying that three times he was beaten with rods, once he was stoned, three times he was shipwrecked. He spent a night and day in the open sea. He experienced times when he went without sleep, and he often went without food and water. Paul even experienced times when he was cold and without clothing. He did not allow situations nor the circumstances of life to defeat him. He learned how to be content with whatever he had (Philippians 4:11). He learned to command the storms in his life. In times of difficulty, he believed that God would rescue him.

On one particular voyage, Paul informed the centurion that the journey would "be with hurt and much damage," (Acts 27:10). Nevertheless, the centurion believed others instead of Paul. When what Paul said came to pass, he said these words, "Wherefore, sirs, be of good cheer: for I believe God, that it shall be even as it was told to me," Acts 27:25. Paul was not guilty, yet he suffered like everyone else aboard the ship because of people who refused to listen to God.

Although the centurion did not listen to Paul's original warning, in the middle of the storm, he followed every instruction that Paul gave him. They had to throw cargo overboard that would cause them to sink. They had to cut away the lifeboat and stay together. After following Paul's instructions, all the soldiers, crew, and prisoners safety made it to shore.

AMERICA IS IN A STORM

America is being torn apart by storms of political, racial, and denominational beliefs. The only way we can all survive as a nation is to turn back to God completely. In John 8:32 (NIV), it says, "Then you will know the truth, and the truth will set you free." The truth is, that Christians must realize what is going on and stay together as a body. We must throw everything contrary to our faith overboard so that God can save our nation and we can move forward in the things of God.

PRAYER TO COMMAND THE STORMS

Dear Heavenly Father, we choose to be free from anything or anyone that has illegally latched on to us. Let us move from all ungodly ways, actions, and thinking. Let us be strong without compromise, or wavering in our faith. Lord, we choose to let go of everything contrary to Your will and purpose for our lives. Thank You, Lord, that You are there in the midst of every storm that we will ever face as You lead, guide, and direct us to safety.

In the name of Jesus, Amen!

CHAPTER 6

MOVING AMERICA FORWARD

"The effectual fervent prayer of a righteous man availeth much."

JAMES 5:16

Have you ever driven in reverse for a long distance? It is very easy to become sidetracked and end up in a ditch. The faster you drive, the more difficulty you have trying to stay in the middle of the road. If you become sidetracked, you tend to move from side to side. If you are not careful, you will end up in a ditch. The same is true in life.

In life, there are many reasons that you can end up in a ditch. One way is by watching the wrong things on television. Television is focused on telling you "their vision." What entertains and what you give your attention to can cause you to catch a different vision. While you are watching and listening to "their vision," you can forget about your vision. You can forget about the vision that God wants for your life.

"Confess your sins to each other and pray for each other so that you may be healed. The earnest prayer of a righteous person has great power and produces wonderful results."

JAMES 5:16 (NLT)

Now is the time to get out of reverse. God is always on the move and always moving forward. He is looking for people that don't want to go in reverse but want to move forward in the spirit realm of God and step to higher heights. He is looking for people that want to move forward with Him.

You have a purpose that God has called you to. In other words, you need to grab a hold of God's vision and quit allowing the enemy to take that vision and do something with it that's not supposed to be done. God wants you to get a hold of the vision He has for your life so you can move forward. Therefore, you need to catch His vision and live accordingly.

THE POWER OF A PRAYING NATION

We, as God's people, need to get serious about praying and not allow ourselves to keep getting into deeper and deeper ditches. We need to pray like never before. It's prayer that's going to make the difference and help us to stay out of the ditches. Prayer is going to keep us out of the ditches of sin.

In James 5:16 (NLT), the Word of God says: "Confess your sins to each other and pray for each other so that you may be healed." The earnest prayer brings prayer power to a righteous person. That kind of prayer has great power and produces wonderful results.

Psalm 91:14-16 (NLT), God said, "I will rescue those who love me. I will protect those who trust in my name. When they call on me, I will answer; I will be with them in trouble. I will rescue and honor them. I will reward them with a long life and give them my salvation." So, we have prayer power if we use it. That is the way to get our eyes of understanding opened unto the supernatural and onto the things of the Lord, through our prayers.

We live in a hurry-up society. A society based on speeding, rushing, and forcing more tasks into our schedules. A society that will make you too tired to go to church, pray with other believers, and spend time with Jesus. It is designed to push Jesus out so that you will not have time to spend with Him.

> "For where two or three are gathered together in my name, there am I in the midst of them."
> Matt 18:20

I remember back when I was growing up, the church was open 24 hours. We could go to the church anytime of the day or night to pray. Because of the continuous prayers going forth to God and the effectual fervent prayer of the righteous, we witnessed massive miracles like Peter and John experienced in the Book of Acts.

> "Now Peter and John went up together into the temple at the hour of prayer, being the ninth hour. And a certain man lame from his mother's womb was car-

ried, whom they laid daily at the gate of the temple which is called Beautiful, to ask alms of them that entered into the temple; Who seeing Peter and John about to go into the temple asked an alms. And Peter, fastening his eyes upon him with John, said, Look on us. And he gave heed unto them, expecting to receive something of them. Acts 3:1-5

The lame man put out the effort to stop Peter and John before they entered the temple. He used his voice to get their attention. He used what he had to get what he did not have. He did not care who heard him. He made his request known. He was determined and ready to receive.

He asked them for money but what he received was a far greater gift. Peter said, "Look at us." He did not want the man to look at his situation. Peter did not want him to focus on the fact that he could not walk nor that he lived in poverty. Peter wanted him to know that God was there to meet his needs if he focused on Jesus.

> Then Peter said, Silver and gold have I none; but such as I have give I thee: In the name of Jesus Christ of Nazareth rise up and walk. And he took him by the right hand, and lifted him up: and immediately his feet and ankle bones received strength. And he leaping up stood, and walked, and entered with them into the temple, walking, and leaping, and praising God." Acts 3:6-8

We must become a nation that is more God-conscious. One of the most important keys to seeing more manifestations of God's power and glory is a person committed to prayer.

> "Now when they saw the boldness of Peter and John, and perceived that they were unlearned and ignorant men, they marvelled; and they took knowledge of them, that they had been with Jesus. And beholding the man which was healed standing with them, they could say nothing against it." Acts 4:13-14

As Americans, if we would spend time in prayer, people will recognize that we have been with Jesus. We will see more miracles happening, the Gospel would spread, the Spirit of God would draw people into the kingdom, and we would continue to *"Have a Jesus Filled America."*

PRAYER FOR AMERICA

Father, in the name of Jesus, we give thanks for America.

Satan, you are not welcome in America. You have no authority in America. We rebuke the devouring spirit of the antichrist and every false god that tries to come and take over the lordship of our lives and this country.

We bind every principality and power of darkness, in the name of Jesus. We bind you in high places and we bind you from taking over and trying to move in or sneak into America. We take authority over you, in the name of Jesus.

We pray that the blinders will come off Christian people and their hearts will not be bound up, and they will see clearly what's taking place. We pray that they will move swiftly in the things of the Holy Ghost. We pray that Christians will take action and stand for what is right, and stand for Jesus.

In Jesus' mighty name, Amen!

CHAPTER 7

PRAYERS
FOR THE
NATION

PRAYER FOR OUR ELECTED OFFICIALS

Father, in the name of Jesus, we lift up our President and every branch of the government. As great decisions are being made that affect us, our children, and the future generations to come, we pray that You give our leaders wisdom and knowledge. Let them stand for righteousness.

We pray that the Holy Ghost will direct them in the things of God, and that this nation will remain as one nation, under God. We make a declaration that we are in faith and unity, believing that You are Lord over America. We declare that whatever changes are needed; that may even mean putting new people in office, so be it. In the name that's above every name.

In the name of Jesus, Amen!

PRAYER FOR CHANGE

Father, in the name of Jesus, we thank You for Your amazing grace, for it endures forever. We ask You to minister through us, for You are the only one that can touch our hearts and lives. We ask that our vessels be used for Your purpose and not our own. We ask for the convicting power of the Holy Ghost to move in such a mighty way, that our hearts will be changed and have a deep desire to pray and seek Your will for America. We ask that the anointing power of the Holy Ghost flow through, on, and over us. Father, we give You the glory and the praise.

In the name of Jesus, Amen!

PRAYER FOR PROTECTION OF THE MILITARY

Father, in the name of Jesus, I thank You for all the men and women in every branch of the military. I give You praise for them. I thank You for what You are doing in their lives by the Spirit of the Living God. I pray that the ministering Spirit of God be disbursed to them right now wherever they are.

Thank You, Lord, that You put someone in their path that will minister to and encourage them. If they don't know You, we pray that they will be convicted of their sins, repent, and give their heart to You.

I pray for Your protection over them. I ask for the safety of Your hand and that the blood of Jesus be upon them and over them. I ask that they have high favor and that they be victorious in every situation in their lives, according to Your Word. Let Your will be done in their lives and the lives of their families. I lift them up to You with thanksgiving and praise. I pray that You are moving on their behalf even right now.

In the name of Jesus, Amen!

PRAYER FOR REVIVAL

Father, in the name of Jesus, we give You thanks that revival is hitting America, the government, the military, the schools, and is spreading across this land. We make a declaration of faith that revival is happening right now. We make a declaration that prayer comes back into schools. We are believing for the Holy Ghost to help this message of salvation to spread.

We stand in agreement that we are going back to the things of God. Father, we give You honor, we give You glory, we give You praise, and we give You thanks. We stand in the gap for this country.

In the name of Jesus, Amen!

PRAYER TO COMMAND THE STORMS

Dear Heavenly Father, we choose to be free from anything or anyone that has illegally latched on to us. Let us move from all ungodly ways, actions, and thinking. Let us be strong without compromise, or wavering in our faith. Lord, we choose to let go of everything contrary to Your will and purpose for our lives. Thank You, Lord, that You are there in the midst of every storm that we will ever face as You lead, guide, and direct us to safety.

In the name of Jesus, Amen!

PRAYER FOR AMERICA

Father, in the name of Jesus, we give thanks for America.

Satan, you are not welcome in America. You have no authority in America. We rebuke the devouring spirit of the antichrist and every false god that tries to come and take over the lordship of our lives and this country.

We bind every principality and power of darkness, in the name of Jesus. We bind you in high places and we bind you from taking over and trying to move in or sneak into America. We take authority over you, in the name of Jesus.

We pray that the blinders will come off Christian people and their hearts will not be bound up, and they will see clearly what's taking place. We pray that they will move swiftly in the things of the Holy Ghost. We pray that Christians will take action and stand for what is right, and stand for Jesus.

In Jesus' mighty name, Amen!

HAVE A
JESUS
FILLED
AMERICA

NOTES

NOTES

NOTES

NOTES

www.ingramcontent.com/pod-product-compliance
Lightning Source LLC
Chambersburg PA
CBHW051006060726
47593CB00017B/1088